AMERICAN CITIES

# CHARLESTON

Eric Reeder

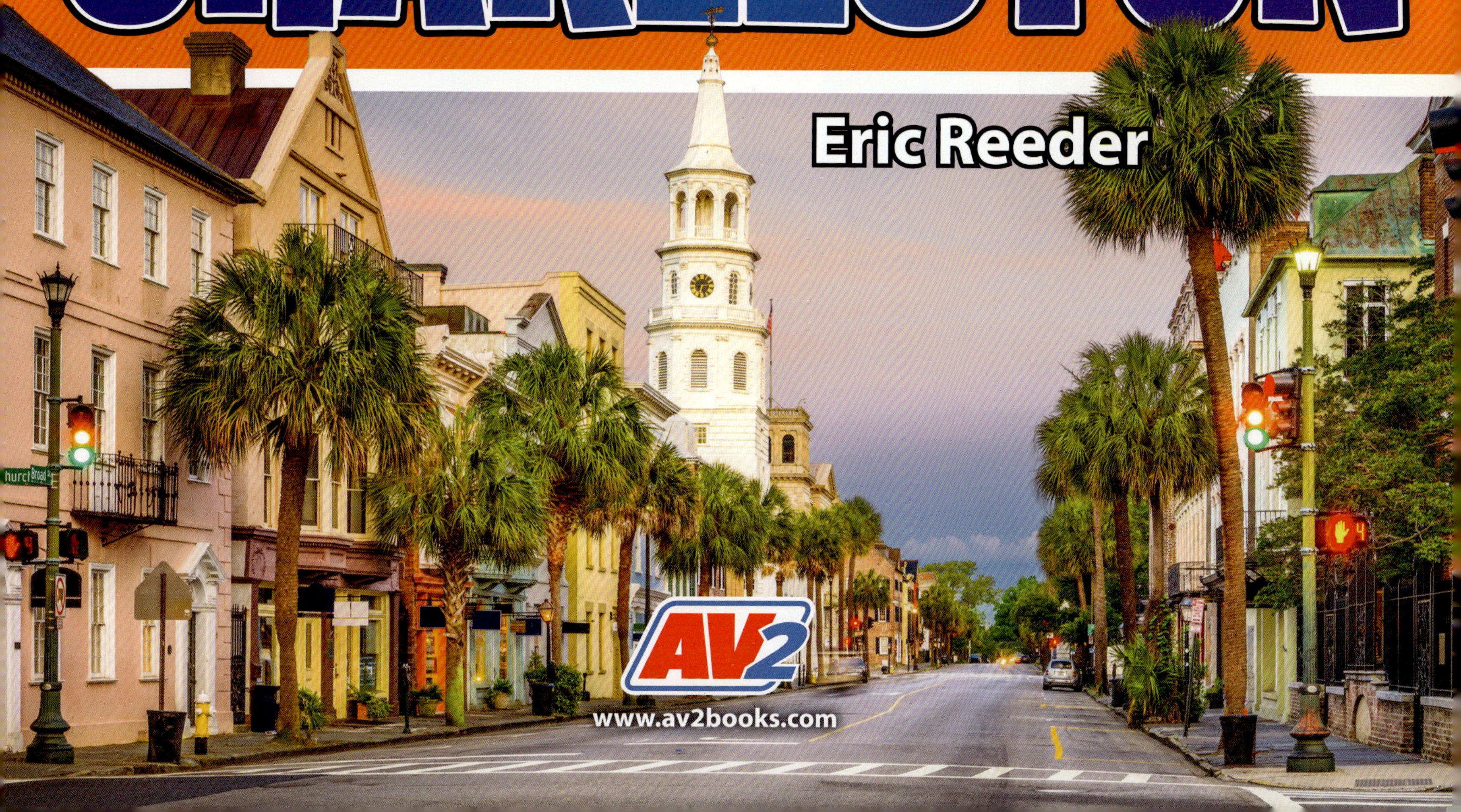

AV2

www.av2books.com

AV2

**Step 1**
Go to **www.av2books.com**

**Step 2**
Enter this unique code
**CNHYI096E**

**Step 3**
Explore your interactive eBook!

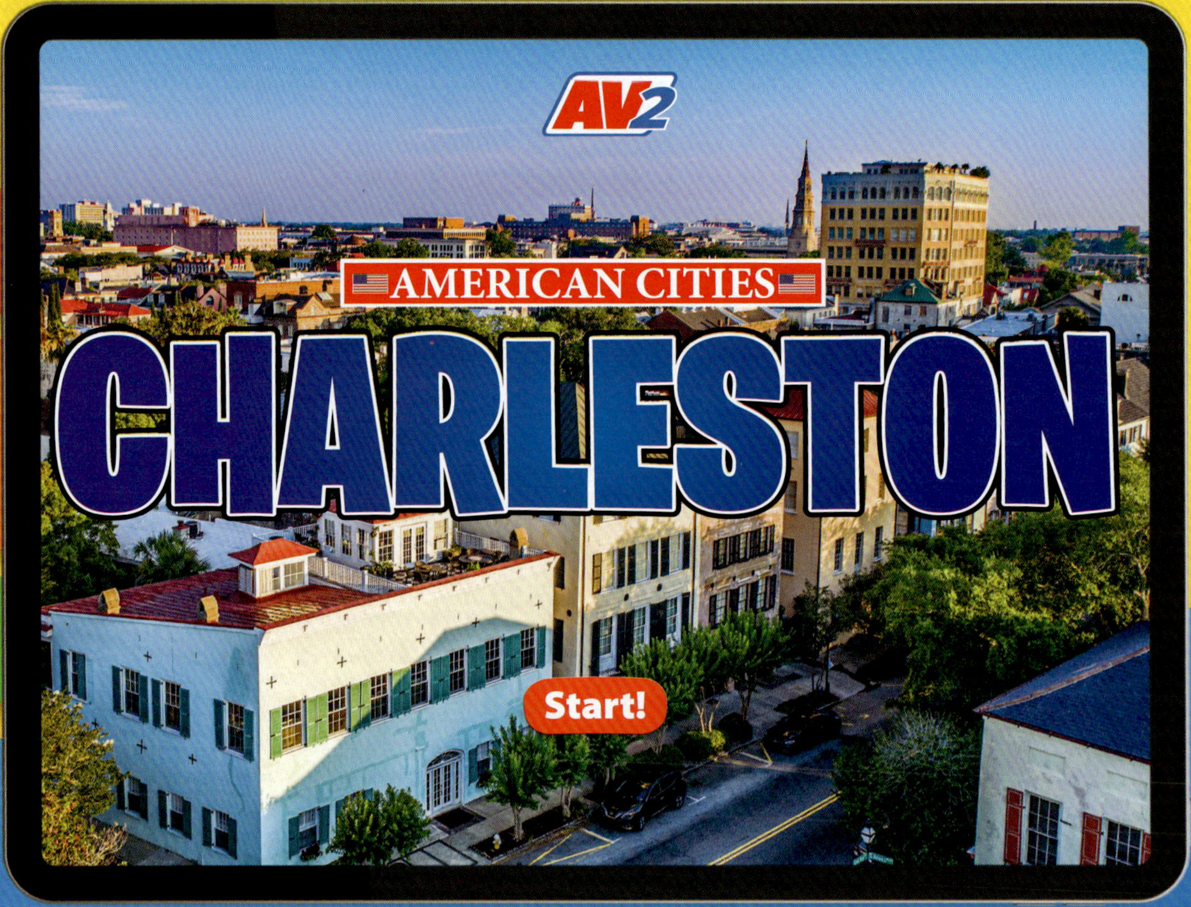


AV2 is optimized for use on any device

## Your interactive eBook comes with...

Read

**Audio**
Listen to the entire book read aloud

**Videos**
Watch informative video clips

**Weblinks**
Gain additional information for research

**Try This!**
Complete activities and hands-on experiments

**Key Words**
Study vocabulary, and complete a matching word activity

**Quizzes**
Test your knowledge

**Slideshows**
View images and captions

**View new titles and product videos at www.av2books.com**

# Contents

# Get to Know Charleston

Charleston is the oldest city in the state of South Carolina. It is sometimes called "The Holy City." This is because it has many churches.

# Map of South Carolina

# Where Is Charleston?

Charleston sits on the coast of the Atlantic Ocean. It is 114 miles southeast of Columbia, the state capital. You can get to Columbia from Charleston by taking the I-26 highway.

There are many other exciting places to visit in South Carolina. You can use a road map to plan a trip. Which roads could you take from Charleston to get to these other places? How long might it take you to get to each place?

| TRAVELING SOUTH CAROLINA |
|---|
| Charleston to Georgetown 61 miles |
| Charleston to Myrtle Beach 95 miles |
| Charleston to Hilton Head Island 98 miles |
| Charleston to Greenville 213 miles |

# Climate

Charleston has a humid, or moist, climate. Its summers are very hot. Winters in the city are mild. Spring and fall are warm. Rain can fall at any time of year. Snow is rare.

Large storms called hurricanes have been known to hit Charleston. They bring high winds and heavy rain. Most hurricanes take place in the summer or early fall.

About **50 inches** of rain falls on Charleston **every year**.

# Population and Geography

More than 136,000 people live in Charleston. Another 650,000 live in the area around the city. Charleston is one of the fastest-growing cities in the country. About 28 people move to or near the city every day.

Charleston was built where three rivers meet. These are the Ashley, Cooper, and Wando Rivers. All three rivers empty into the Atlantic Ocean.

# Many Peoples

Aboriginal Peoples were the first to live where Charleston is today. English settlers arrived in 1670. These people built a town on the land. They called it Charles Towne. It was named for England's king. The name was changed to Charleston in 1783.

Charleston grew quickly. By 1800, almost 20,000 people lived in the city. Charleston was an important port. Goods such as rice and cotton shipped from there.

In **1800**, Charleston was the **fifth-largest** city in the United States.

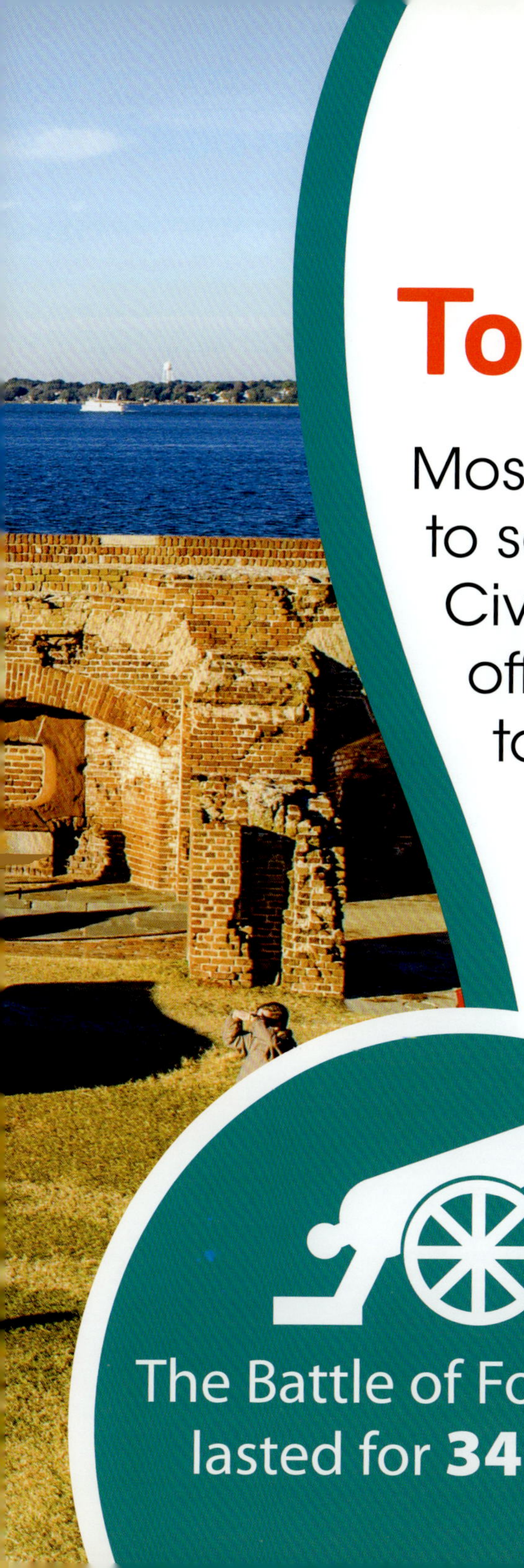

# Tourism

Most visitors to Charleston take time to see Fort Sumter. It was there that the Civil War began. The fort sits on an island off the coast. People take a boat ride to get there.

The Battery is another popular place to visit. This walkway stretches along the Charleston waterfront. It is one of the best places to see the city's grand houses.

The Battle of Fort Sumter lasted for **34 hours.**

# Sports

Charleston has two main sports teams. The Charleston RiverDogs are the city's main baseball team. They play their home games in Joseph P. Riley, Jr. Park. The Charleston Battery is the city's main soccer team. Their home field is on Daniel Island.

The city also has several college sports teams. The Citadel Bulldogs and the Charleston Southern Buccaneers are two of the best known. Both teams play football.

THE Q
GAME NETWORK
13
2

# Economy

Tourism is big business for Charleston. Each year, more than 7 million people come to the city. They spend money on hotels and food.

Charleston has a busy port. Every year, goods worth about $70 million are shipped through the city. These goods include car parts and lumber.

In **2018**, tourism brought more than **$8 billion** to the city.

# Charleston Timeline

**50,000 years ago**
Aboriginal Peoples live in the Charleston area.

**1670**
English settlers arrive and found the settlement of Charles Towne.

**1780**
The British launch an attack on the city as part of the American Revolution.

**1783**
The Americans win the Revolution, and the city is renamed Charleston.

**1861**
The first shots of the Civil War are fired at Fort Sumter.

**1989**
Hurricane Hugo damages many of Charleston's historic buildings.

**1886**
A major earthquake hits Charleston. It kills more than 100 people.

**2019**
Charleston is named the best city in the United States to visit.

# Things to Do in Charleston

**Charles Towne Landing State Historic Site**

Charles Towne was founded on this exact spot in 1670. Visitors can watch cannons being fired and tour a tall ship.

**Children's Museum of the Lowcountry**

This museum provides hands-on activities for children. They can get creative in a Medieval castle and build an airplane all in one visit.

## Patriots Point Naval and Maritime Museum

Visitors to this museum can tour a variety of military ships, including an aircraft carrier. They can even see what it is like to be a fighter pilot.

## Magnolia Plantation and Gardens

Built in 1676, this is one of the oldest plantations, or farms, in the South. People can tour the plantation house and take a train ride around the grounds.

## South Carolina Aquarium

This aquarium is home to 5,000 animals. They include birds, alligators, turtles, and sharks.

# KEY WORDS

Research has shown that as much as 65 percent of all written material published in English is made up of 300 words. These 300 words cannot be taught using pictures or learned by sounding them out. They must be recognized by sight. This book contains 111 common sight words to help young readers improve their reading fluency and comprehension. This book also teaches young readers several important content words, such as proper nouns. These words are paired with pictures to aid in learning and improve understanding.

| Page | Sight Words First Appearance |
|---|---|
| 4 | get, know, to |
| 5 | because, city, has, in, is, it, many, of, sometimes, state, the, this |
| 7 | a, are, by, can, could, each, from, how, long, might, miles, on, other, places, take, there, these, use, where, which, you |
| 8 | about, and, any, at, been, every, have, high, its, large, most, or, they, time, very, year |
| 11 | all, another, around, country, day, into, live, more, move, near, one, people, rivers, than, three, was |
| 12 | almost, an, as, changed, first, for, goods, important, land, named, such, were |
| 15 | along, began, houses, off, see, that |
| 16 | also, both, home, play, their, two |
| 19 | big, car, come, food, parts, through |
| 20 | Americans, found |
| 22 | children, do, hands, things, watch |
| 23 | animals, be, even, farms, like, what |

| Page | Content Words First Appearance |
|---|---|
| 4 | Charleston |
| 5 | churches, South Carolina |
| 7 | Atlantic Ocean, coast, Columbia, highway, map, roads, trip |
| 8 | climate, fall, hurricanes, inches, rain, snow, spring, storms, summers, winds, winters |
| 11 | area, Ashley, Cooper, geography, population, Wando |
| 12 | Aboriginal Peoples, Charles Towne, cotton, king, port, rice, settlers, town, United States |
| 15 | Battery, Battle of Fort Sumter, Civil War, Fort Sumter, hours, island, ride, tourism, visitors, walkway, waterfront |
| 16 | Charleston Battery, Charleston RiverDogs, Charleston Southern Buccaneers, Citadel Bulldogs, Daniel Island, field, football, games, Joseph P. Riley Jr. Park, sports, teams |
| 19 | business, economy, hotels, lumber, money |
| 20 | American Revolution, attack, British, settlement, timeline |
| 21 | buildings, earthquake, Hurricane Hugo, shots |
| 22 | activities, airplane, castle, cannons, Charles Towne Landing State Historic Site, Children's Museum of the Lowcountry, ship, spot, visit |
| 23 | aircraft carrier, alligators, birds, grounds, Magnolia Plantation and Gardens, Patriots Point Maritime and Naval Museum, pilot, sharks, South Carolina Aquarium, turtles, variety |

Published by AV2
350 5th Avenue, 59th Floor New York, NY 10118
Website: www.av2books.com



Library of Congress Cataloging-in-Publication Data
Names: Reeder, Eric, author.
Title: Charleston / Eric Reeder and Heather Kissock.
Description: New York, NY : AV2, [2020] | Series: American cities | Audience: Ages 6-9 | Audience: Grades 2-3 |
Summary: "American Cities takes young readers on a tour of our capitals and major centers. Each book explores the geography, history, and people that give the featured city its distinctive flair."-- Provided by publisher.
Identifiers: LCCN 2019042738 (print) | LCCN 2019042739 (ebook) | ISBN 9781791115869 (library binding) | ISBN 9781791115876 (paperback) | ISBN 9781791115883 | ISBN 9781791115890
Subjects: LCSH: Charleston (S.C.)--Juvenile literature.
Classification: LCC F279.C44 R44 2020 (print) | LCC F279.C44 (ebook) | DDC 975.7/915--dc23
LC record available at https://lccn.loc.gov/2019042738
LC ebook record available at https://lccn.loc.gov/2019042739

Printed in Guangzhou, China
1 2 3 4 5 6 7 8 9 0 24 23 22 21 20

012020
100919

Project Coordinator: Heather Kissock Designer: Ana María Vidal

AV2 acknowledges Getty Images, Alamy, Newscom, Shutterstock, and Wikimedia as the primary image suppliers for this title.